STARTER

T0350551

PUPIL'S BOOK

Leone Dyson

Pearson Education Limited
Edinburgh Gate
Harlow
Essex CM20 2JE
England
and Associated Companies throughout the world.

www.islands.pearson.com

First published 2012

ISBN: 978-1-4479-2470-8

Set in Fiendstar Bold

Illustrated by Ilias Arahovitis (Beehive Illustration), Abraham Balcázar and José Luis Briseño.

Printed in China
CTPSC/05

Photo Acknowledgements
The publisher would like to thank the following for their kind permission to reproduce their photographs:

(Key: b-bottom; c-centre; l-left; r-right; t-top)

Alamy Images: David R. Frazier Photolibrary, Inc. 33 (taxi), Peter Jordan_NE 33 (school), Peter Titmuss 33 (bus), T.M.O.Buildings 33 (shop); **Fotolia.com:** Joanna Zielinska 57l, Mariusz Blach 59 (mango); **Getty Images:** Comstock 39r; **iStockphoto:** reanas 41 (shirt); **Pearson Education Inc:** 15 (boy playing), 15 (boy reading), 15 (classroom), 15 (computer room), 15 (laptop), 15 (music classroom), 15 (playground), 15 (singing), 19, 21l, 21r, 23 (artist), 23 (Astronaut), 23 (dentist), 23 (doctor), 23 (firefighter), 23 (nurse), 23 (policeman), 23 (vet), 27, 29l, 29r, 33 (fire station), 33 (hospital), 33 (post office), 37, 39l, 41 (dress), 41 (jacket), 41 (jeans), 41 (jumper), 41 (shoes), 41 (skirt), 41 (socks), 45, 47l, 47r, 51 (angry), 51 (excited), 51 (happy), 51 (hungry), 51 (sad), 51 (scared), 51 (thirsty), 55, 57r, 59 (banana), 59 (carrot), 59 (fork), 59 (luttuce), 59 (orange), 59 (plate), 59 (tomato), 63, 65l, 65r, 67 (Banana), 67 (Luttuce), 67 (Orange), 67 (Tomato), 69 (Bat), 69 (bear), 69 (elephant), 69 (lion), 69 (monkey), 69 (penguin), 69 (sea lion), 69 (zebra), 73, 75l, 75r, 77 (building), 77 (field), 77 (flat), 77 (forest), 77 (mountain), 77 (river), 77 (street), 77 (traffic light), 81, 83l, 83r, 87, 91, 93, 95, 97, 99, 101

Every effort has been made to trace the copyright holders and we apologise in advance for any unintentional omissions. We would be pleased to insert the appropriate acknowledgement in any subsequent edition of this publication.

Contents

Welcome

4

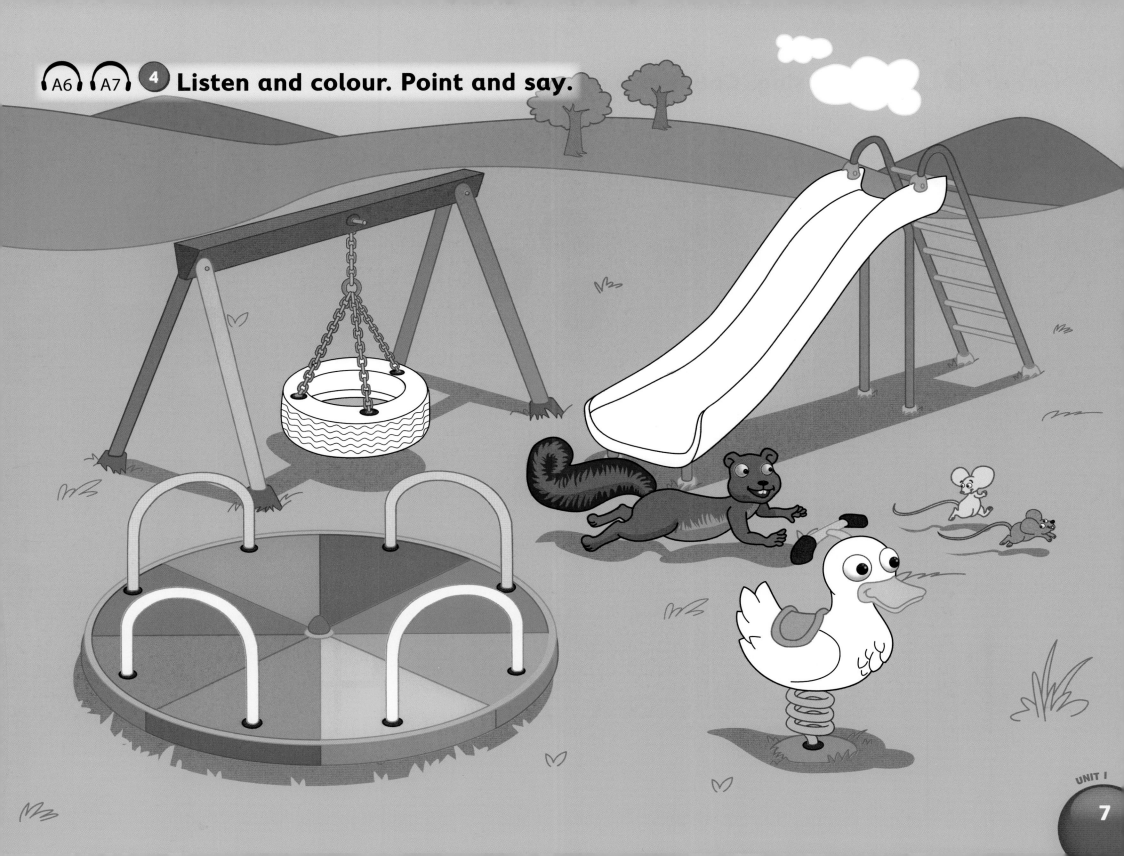

A6 A7 4 **Listen and colour. Point and say.**

UNIT 1

7

♪ **5** **Listen and sing. Count and match.** SONG

1 2 3 4 5

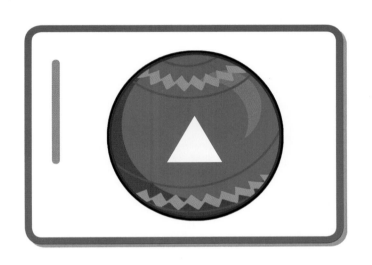

1

2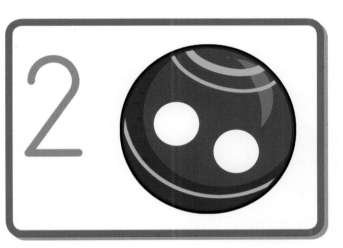

3

4

5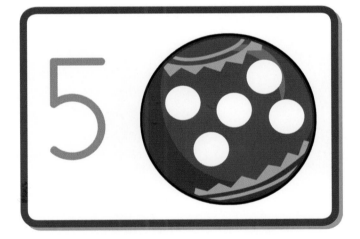

How many?

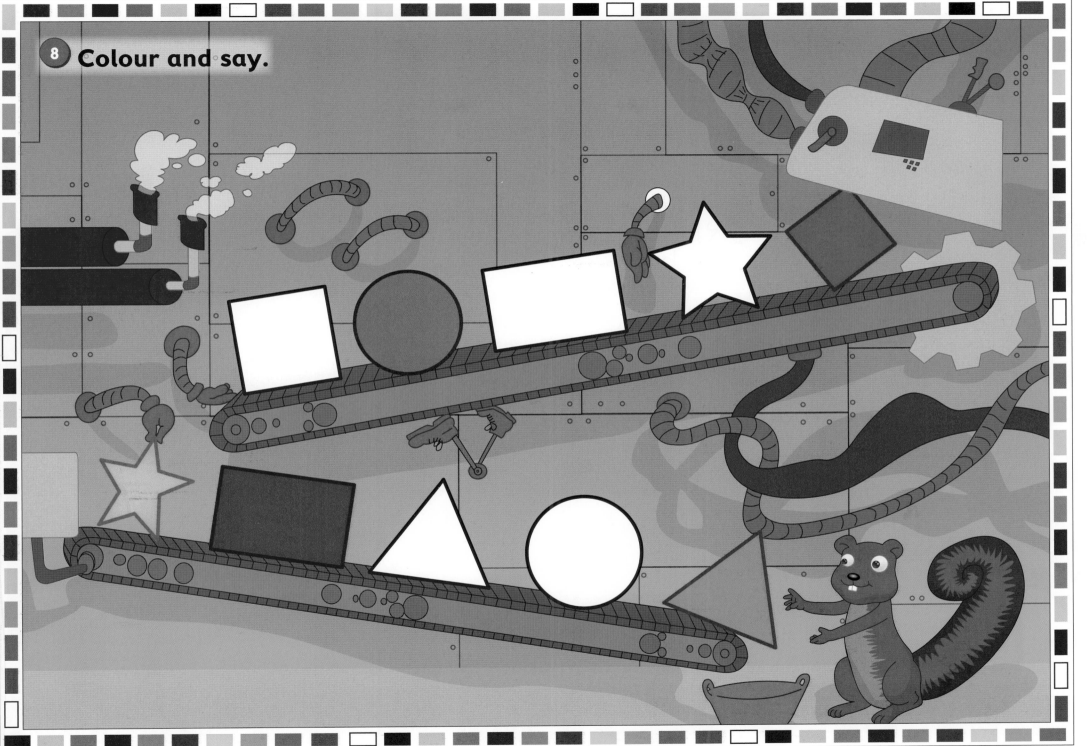

8 Colour and say.

Who's she?

She's my aunt.

2 At School

classroom

read

computer room

use the computer

playground

play

sing

music room

A15 **2** **Listen and number. Say.**

1

8

My School

LISTENING

 A17 **4** **Listen and match. Write.**

1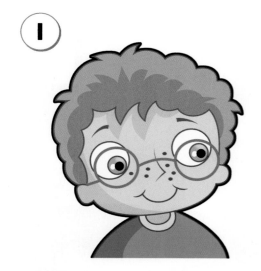

2

3

4

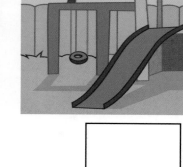

 1

SPEAKING

EXTRA PRACTICE Page 87

5 **Ask and answer. Circle.**

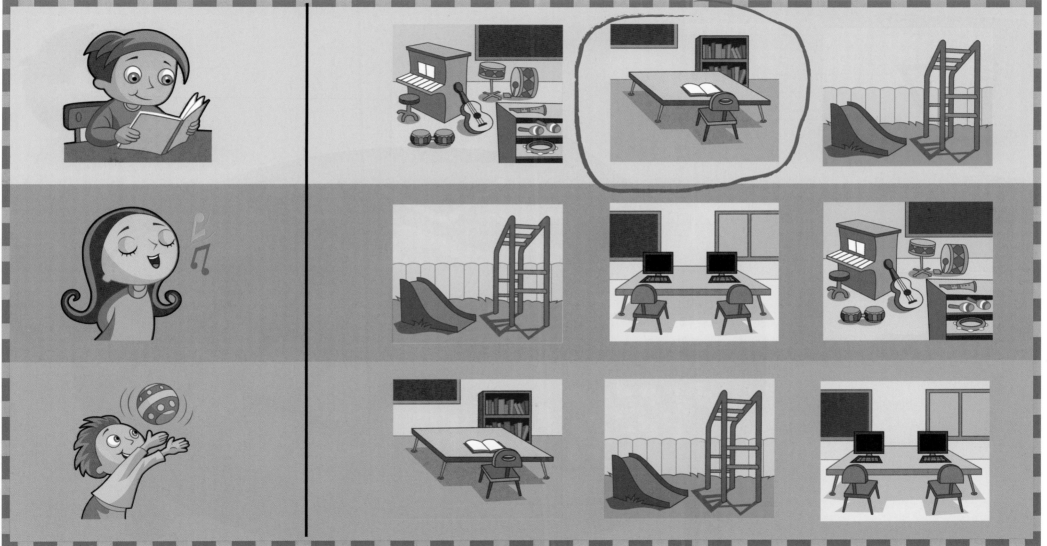

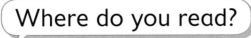

Where do you read?

In the classroom.

A18 6 **Listen, say, and trace. Count and write.** SONG

7 _____

_____

_____

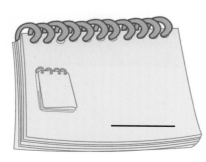

_____

VALUES

3 Workers

Parade day!

vet

nurse

dentist

doctor

astronaut

police officer

firefighter

artist

FIRE

22

VOCABULARY

2 **Listen and number. Say.**

A22 3 **Look and listen. Act it out.**

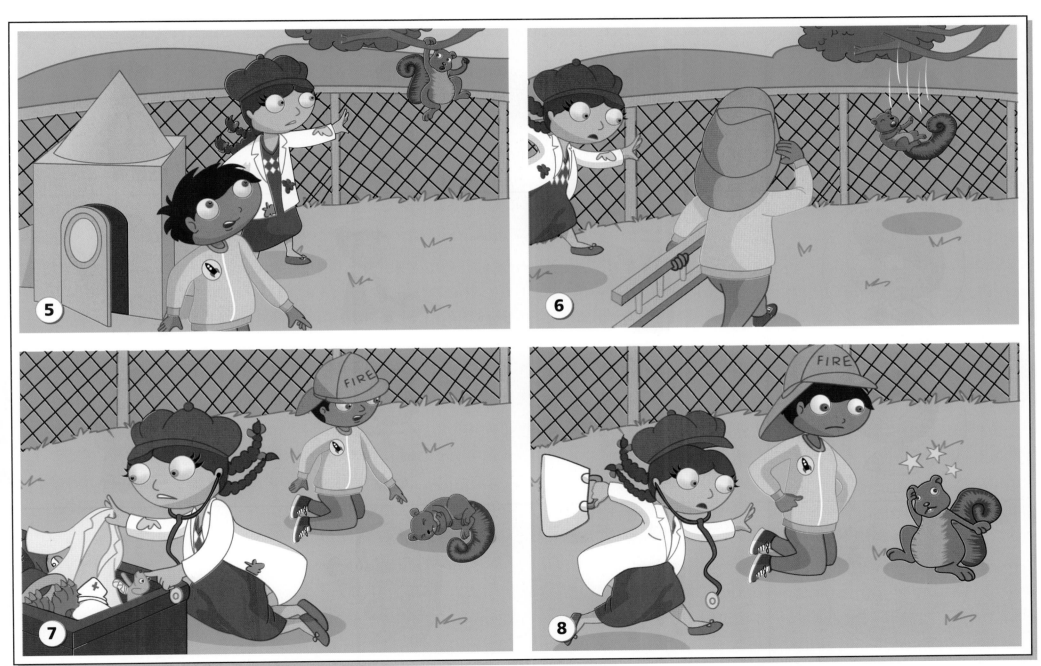

1			
2			
3			
4			

5 Choose and draw. Ask and answer.

What do you want to be?

I want to be a doctor.

CLIL

A24 6 Listen, say, and trace. Count and write. SONG

9 10 11 12

VALUES

UNIT 2 REVIEW

1 **Stick and say.** A26 **2** **Listen and circle.**

1

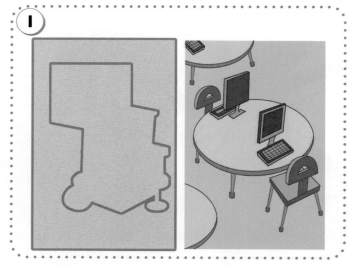

2

3

4

Project

Our school

Unit 2
GOOD
JOB!

UNIT 3 REVIEW

3 Stick and say. A27 **4** Listen and circle.

1

2

3

4

⚠ Project

danger!

Unit 3
GOOD
JOB!

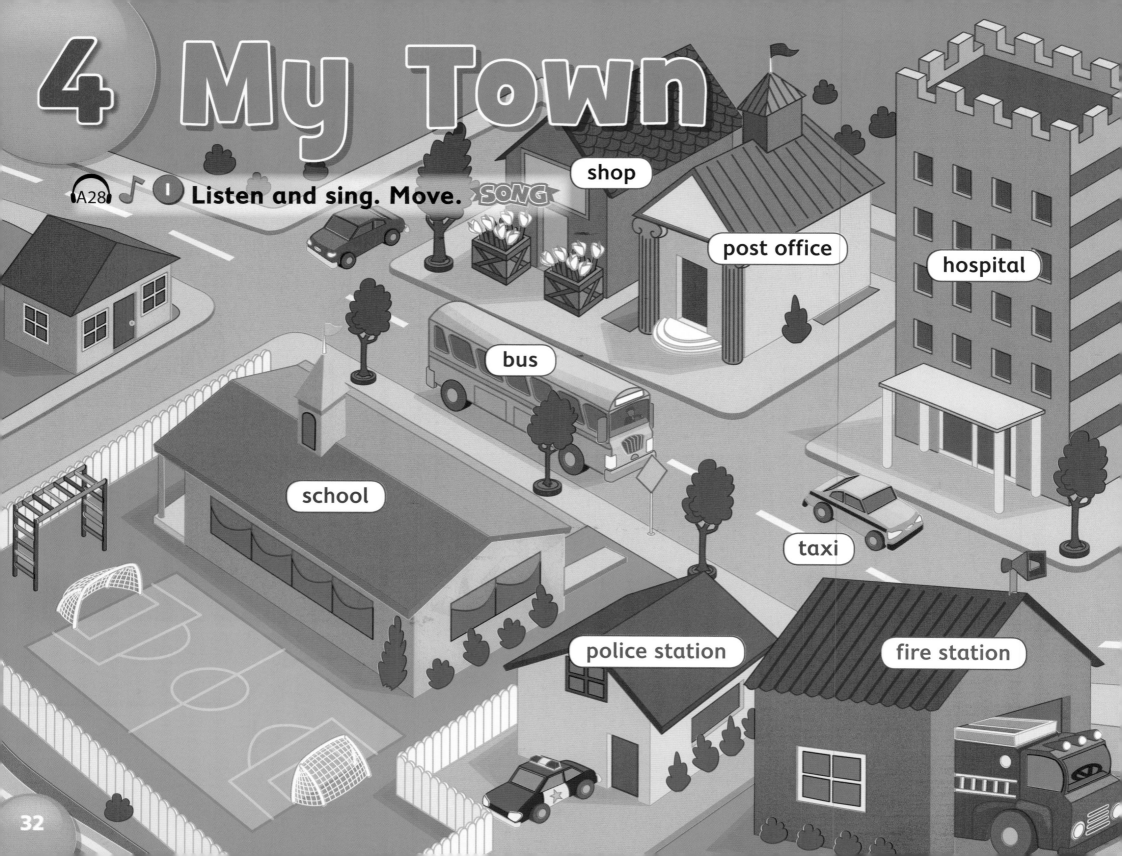

4 My Town

A28 1 Listen and sing. Move. SONG

shop

post office

hospital

bus

school

taxi

police station

fire station

32

VOCABULARY

A29 **2** **Listen and number. Say.**

1

Where Does He Work?

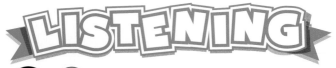

LISTENING

A31 4 **Listen and circle.**

1
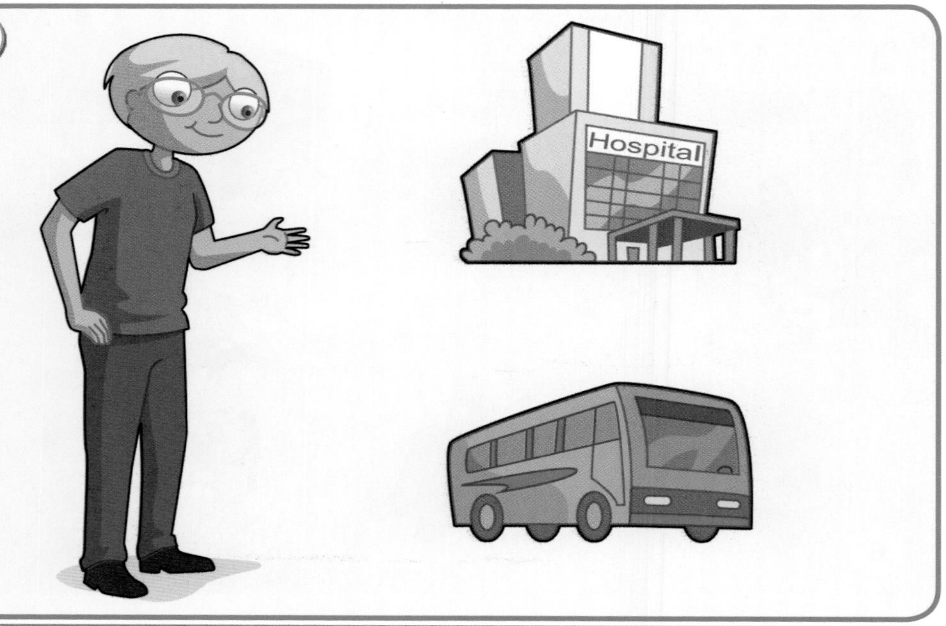

2
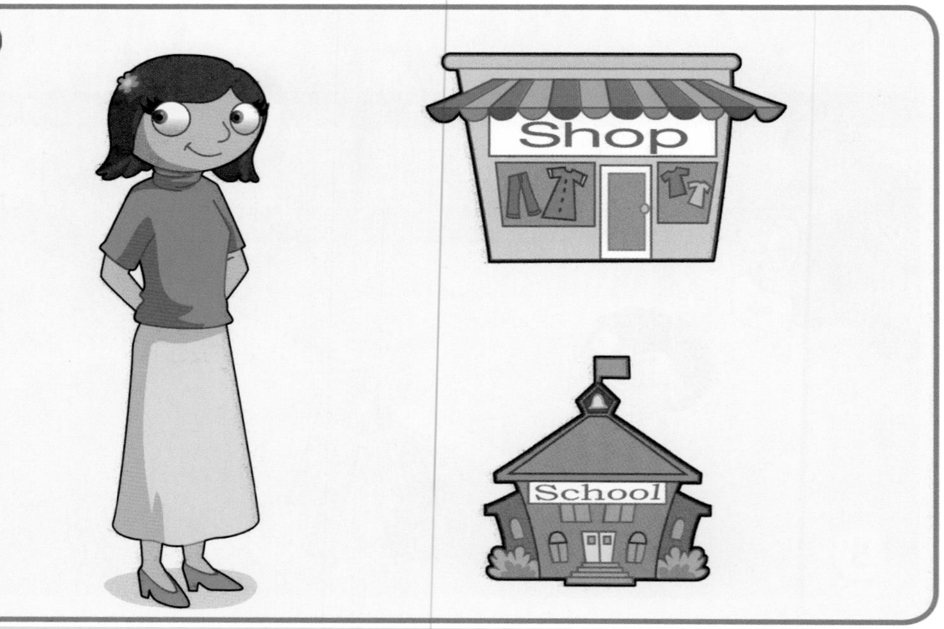

3
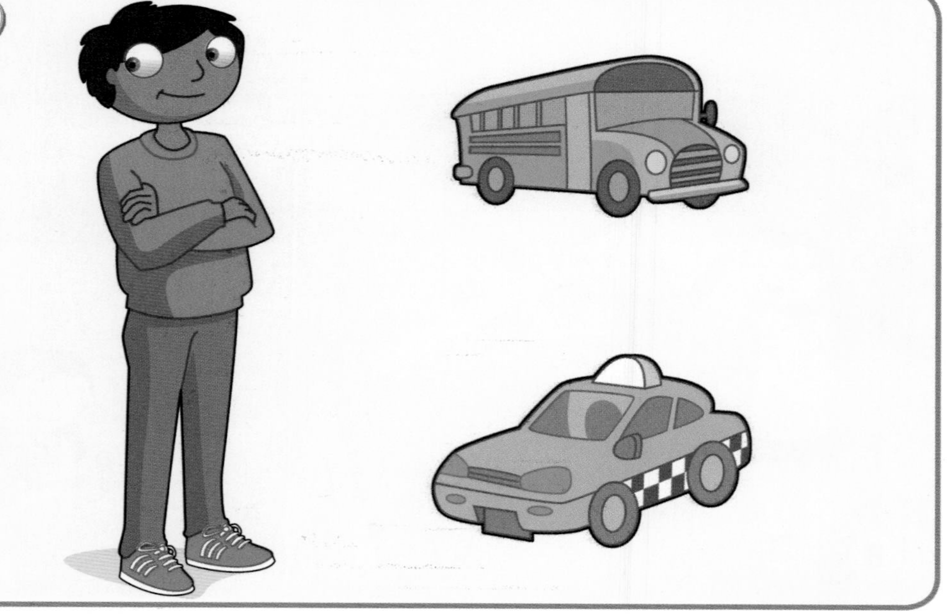

4
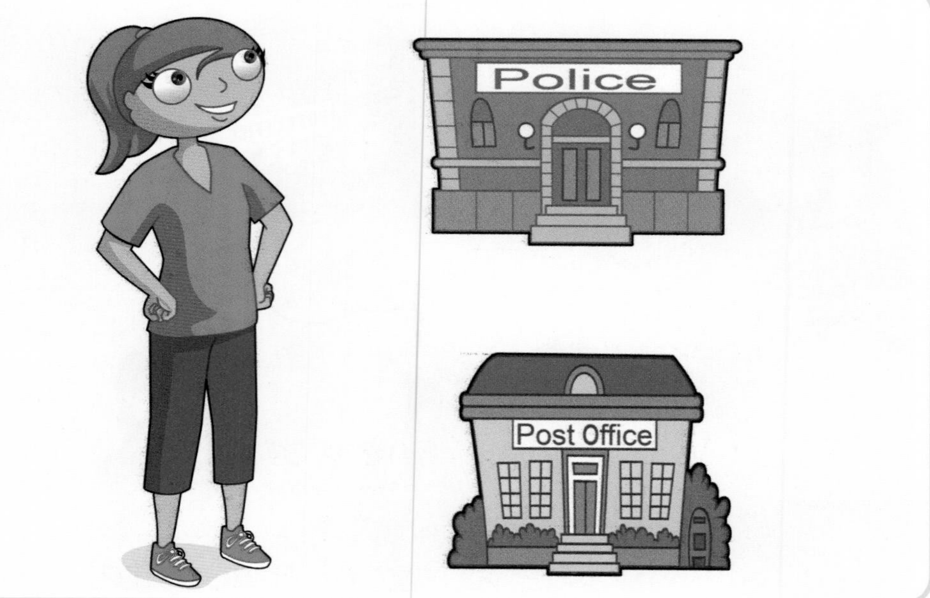

SPEAKING

5 **Match. Ask and answer.**

1

2

3

4

Police

Hospital

Fire Station

School

Where does she work?

She works at a hospital.

A32 6 Listen, say, and trace. Count and write. SONG

11 12 13 14

38

5 Clothes

A34 🎵 **1** Listen and sing. Move. SONG

jacket

sweater

shirt

skirt

trousers

dress

socks

shoes

40

VOCABULARY

2 **Listen and number. Say.**

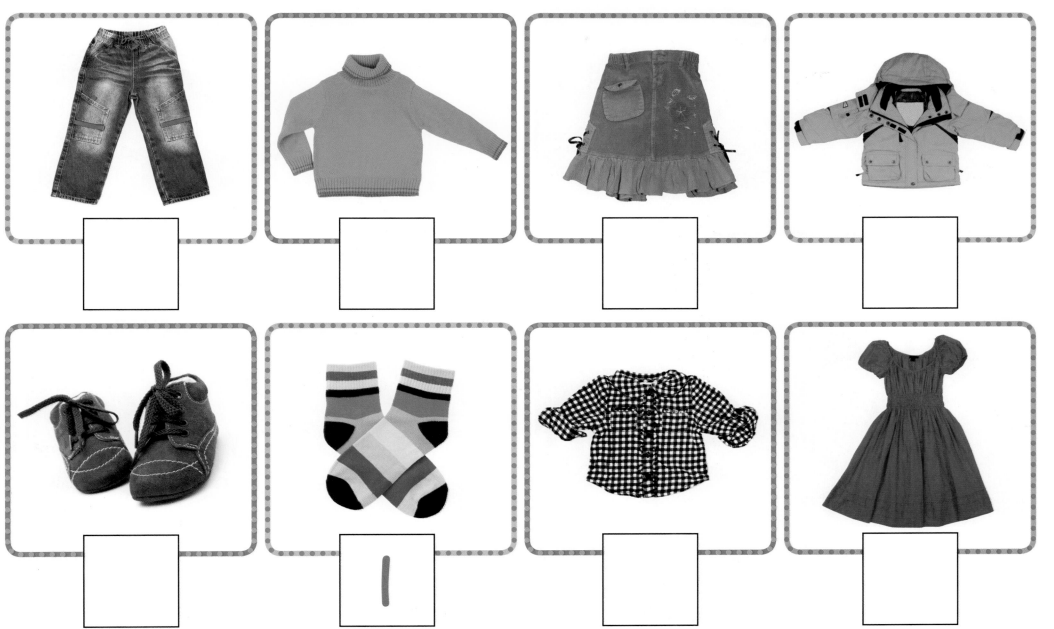

	1

The Holiday

A36 3 **Look and listen. Act it out.**

A37 **4** **Listen and find. Then write.**

46

VALUES

UNIT 4 REVIEW

1 Stick and say. A40 **2** Listen and circle.

1

2

3

4
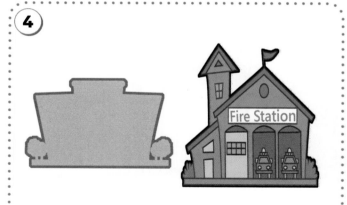

1+2=3 **Project**

Unit 4
GOOD
JOB!

UNIT 5 REVIEW

3 Stick and say. (A41) **4** Listen and circle.

1

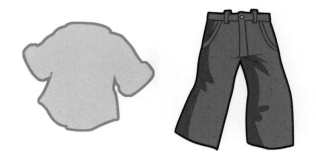

2

3

4

I ♥

I ♥

Unit 5
GOOD
JOB!

6 Feelings

excited

happy

angry

scared

tired

sad

hungry

thirsty

50

2 Listen and number. Say.

 **The Ride**

3 **Look and listen. Act it out.**

LISTENING

SPEAKING

 EXTRA PRACTICE
Page 95

5 Match, ask, and answer.

 How does Lou feel?

He's excited!

A46 6 **Listen, say, and trace. Count and write.** SONG

15 16 17 18

VALUES

7 Healthy Food

fork

carrot

banana

mango

plate

lettuce

orange

tomato

58

B2 **2** **Listen and number. Say.**

At the Market

5

6

7

8

Ask and answer. Tick ✔.

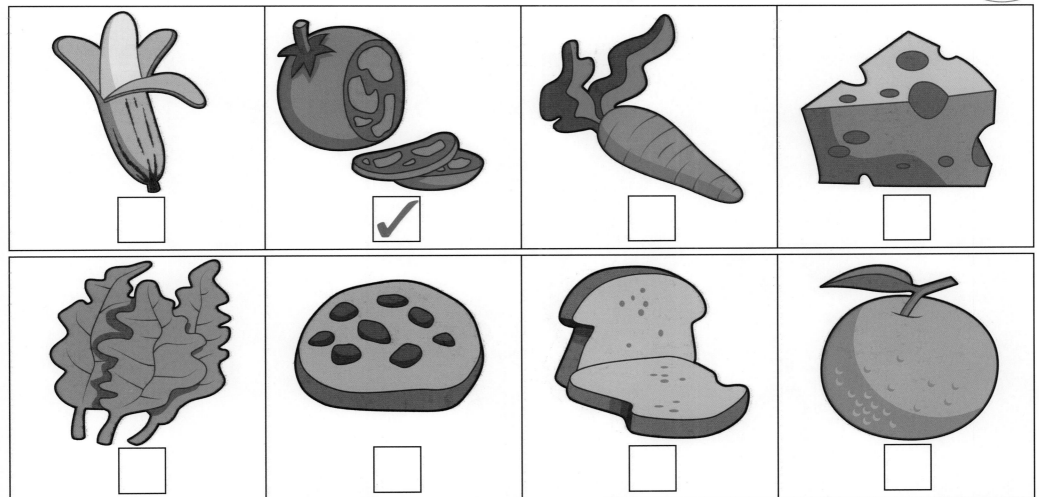

What do you want?

I want a tomato, please.

CLIL

B5 **6** **Listen, say, and trace.**
Count and write. SONG

UNIT 6 REVIEW

1

2

3

4

Project

happy

excited

scared

Unit 6
GOOD
JOB!

UNIT 7 REVIEW

3 Stick and say. B8 **4** Listen and circle.

1
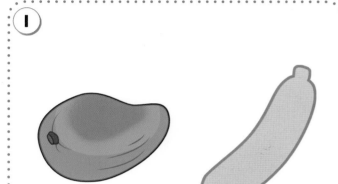

2

3
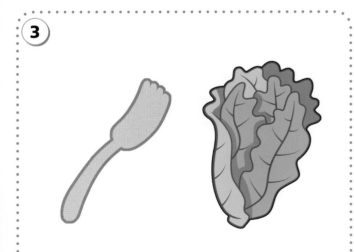

4

Project

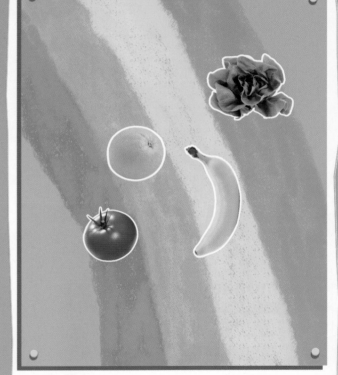

Unit 7 GOOD JOB!

8 The Zoo

lion

elephant

zebra

bear

monkey

sea lion

penguin

bat

68

VOCABULARY

2 **Listen and number. Say.**

What's That?

LISTENING

START

72

5 Ask and answer. Number.

EXTRA PRACTICE
Page 99

What's that?

It's a big sea lion.

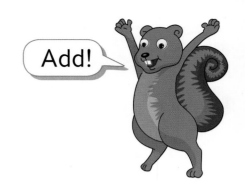

Add!

 +  =

  +  =

   + 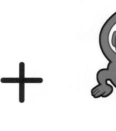 =

 +   =

9 Places

1 **Listen and sing. Move.** SONG

mountain

forest

tree

field

river

building

flat

traffic light

street

76

VOCABULARY

2 **Listen and number. Say.**

Where Do Bears Live?

3 **Look and listen. Act it out.**

LISTENING

SPEAKING

EXTRA PRACTICE
Page 101

5 **Match animals to homes. Ask and answer.**

1

2

3

4

5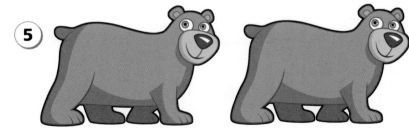

Where do ducks live?

They live in the river.

UNIT 9

81

Take away!

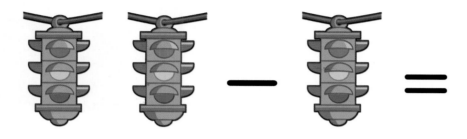

B20 7 **Listen and say. Draw.**

1 Stick and say. B21 **2** Listen and circle.

1

2

3

4

Project

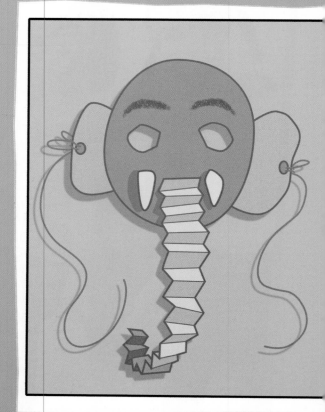

Unit 8 GOOD JOB!

UNIT 9 REVIEW

3 Stick and say. B22 **4** Listen and circle.

1

2
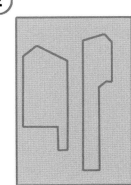 

3
 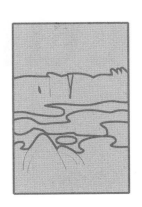

4
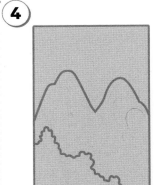 

Project

NO X

YES ✓

Unit 9 GOOD JOB!

PHONICS

Give me a c!

B23 **Listen, match and say.** SONG   B24 **Now listen and say the sounds.**

c

h

j

hen

car

jump

EXTRA PRACTICE

Match. Ask and answer.

Where do you sing?

In the music room.

Give me a *q*!

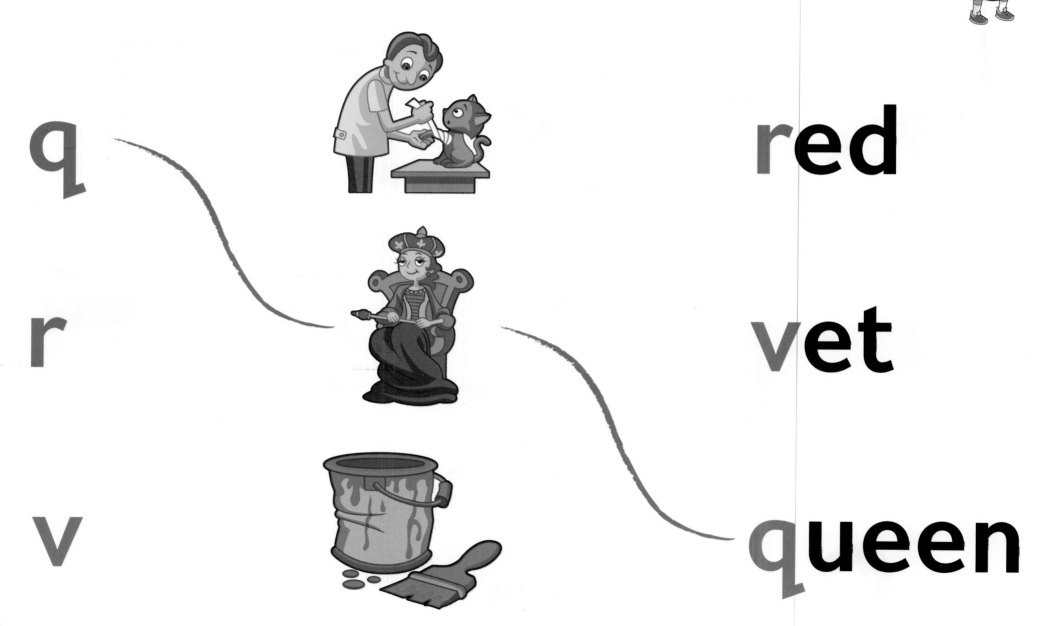

q

r

v

red

vet

queen

EXTRA PRACTICE

Look and draw. Say.

I want to be an artist.

Give me a *w!*

w

windy

x

bo**x**

y

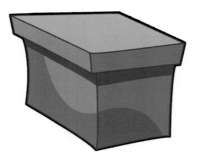

yellow

EXTRA PRACTICE

Match and say. Ask and answer.

1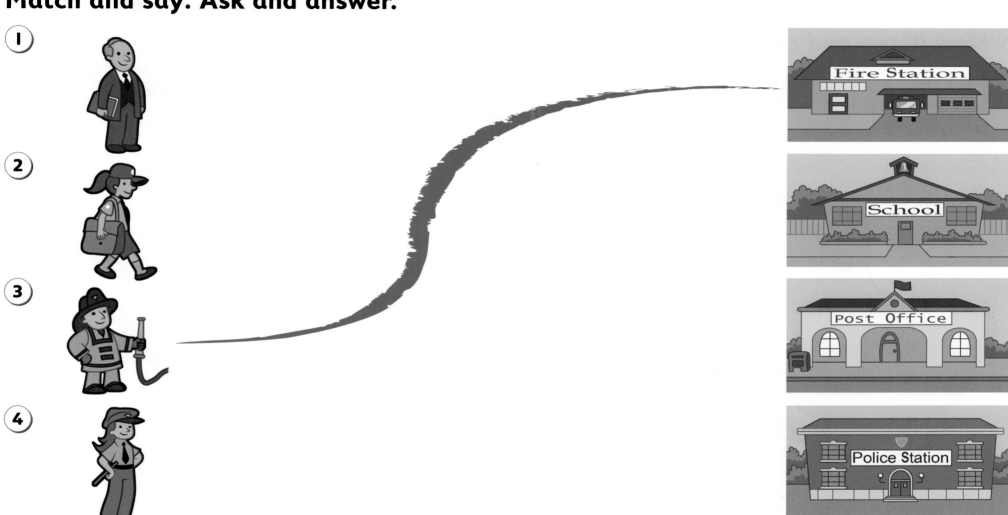

2

3

4

One. Where does he work?

He works at a fire station.

PHONICS

Give me an e!

B29 **Listen, match and say.** SONG

B30 **Now listen and clap if you hear an e sound.**

e

bed

pen

hen

 **PHONICS**

 **Listen, match and say.** **SONG**

B32 Now listen and clap if you hear an *a* sound.

Give me an *a*!

a

cat

dad

hand

Ask and answer.

 **PHONICS**

(B33) **Listen, match and say.** SONG

(B34) **Now listen and clap if you hear an o sound.**

Give me an *o*!

 o

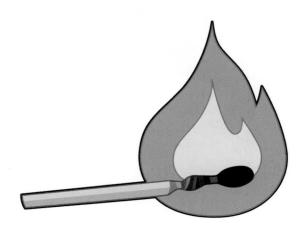

hot

doll

box

EXTRA PRACTICE

Ask and answer.

1

2

3

4

5

6

7

One. What do you want? I want a carrot, please.

 **PHONICS**

Give me a *u*!

(B35) **Listen, match and say.** SONG

(B36) **Now listen and clap if you hear an *u* sound.**

u

sun

cup

bus

EXTRA PRACTICE

Ask and answer.

 PHONICS

B37 **Listen, match and say.** SONG

B38 **Now listen and clap if you hear an _i_ sound.**

Give me an _i_!

i

sit

fish

milk

EXTRA PRACTICE

Match. Ask and answer.

 Where do goats live?

 They live in the mountains.

FESTIVALS New Year

B39 ♪ Cut and stick. Sing. SONG

Cutouts on page 107

HAPPY NEW YEAR!

102

FESTIVALS Easter

B41 ♪ **Colour the eggs. Cut and stick. Sing.** SONG

Cutouts on page 10

FESTIVALS Easter

Follow the paths. Cut and stick.

Cutouts on page III

Congratulations!

_____

has finished Islands Starter.

CUTOUTS

Cut out one or more for page 102.

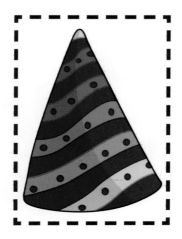

Cut out one or more for page 103.

HAPPY VALENTINE'S DAY

Cut out one or more for page 104.

Cut out for page 105.

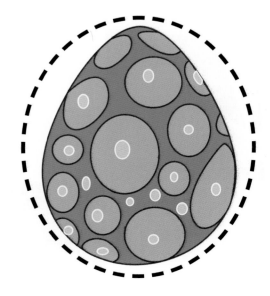